D0946718

WITHDRAWN

RALPH WALDO EMERSON:

His Maternal Ancestors.

Ruth Emerson.

RALPH WALDO EMERSON

HIS MATERNAL ANCESTORS

WITH

Some Reminiscences of Him

BY

DAVID GREENE HASKINS, D.D.

KENNIKAT PRESS
Port Washington, N. Y./London

KENNIKAT PRESS SCHOLARLY REPRINTS

Dr. Ralph Adams Brown, Senior Editor

Series on
LITERARY AMERICA IN THE NINETEENTH CENTURY
Under the General Editorial Supervision of
Dr. Walter Harding
University Professor, State University of New York

RALPH WALDO EMERSON
HIS MATERNAL ANCESTORS

First published in 1887
Reissued in 1971 by Kennikat Press
Library of Congress Catalog Card No: 76-122656
ISBN 0-8046-1305-2

Manufactured in the United States of America

PUBLISHERS' PREFACE.

THE substance of this volume originally appeared, as serial papers, in the August and September numbers for 1886 of *The Literary World*. From the types of this periodical, a small pamphlet edition of these papers — only three hundred and fifty copies — was made up and issued by the present publishers. The continued demand for the pamphlet has led to the publication of it in a more permanent form.

In this edition much new material, mostly derived from family sources, has been supplied by the author, who was Mr. Emerson's cousin. The volume has

also

also been illustrated by represen-
tations of some persons and
places intimately connected or
associated with Mr. Emerson.
Of the illustrations, some have
never before been made public.

INTRODUCTORY.

THE biographies of Mr. Ralph Waldo Emerson which have thus far appeared do not include an account of his mother's family.

Believing that the public is interested in whatever relates to him, and having in my possession the more important papers necessary for giving the history of the family on his mother's side, I have undertaken in these pages, in some measure, to make good the omission.

I have also ventured to supplement the record by some personal reminiscences of Mr. Emerson. If any one else had been able to throw these recollections upon the screen, I certainly should not have taken it upon

myself

myself to do it. The reader will bear in mind that I had been unconsciously photographed into the negatives, and could not eliminate myself from the copies. In exhibiting these views to the public, I defer to the wishes of friends in whose judgment I have confidence.

CONTENTS.

Publisher's Preface   v
Introductory   vii
Robert Haskins   2
John Haskins   3
King's Chapel   15
Hannah Haskins   28
Ruth (Haskins) Emerson   38
Madam Bradford's Letter   53
Mrs. Ruth Emerson's Letters about her
    son, John Clarke   65
Ralph Haskins   80
The Canterbury House   86
Edward B. Emerson   87
Henry F. Harrington   92
" Good-by, proud world "   97
Reminiscences of R. W. Emerson . . 107
School in Roxbury 109
Grace before Meat 114
His Method of Composing 115
His Religious Beliefs 117
Henry D. Thoreau 119

His Explanation of Carlisle's Style . 123
Letter about Gibbon 125
Answer to the Question, "Do you be-
    lieve in God?" 130
Miss Martineau 131
His Funeral 134
Concluding Remarks 136
Notes 143

ILLUSTRATIONS.

1. Ruth Emerson, mother of Ralph
    Waldo Emerson . . . *Frontispiece*
2. Ralph Waldo Emerson,
                    Title-page vignette
3. John Haskins (portrait), facing page   3
4. The Haskins House . .   "   "   8
5. King's Chapel . . . .   "   "   15
6. John Haskins (silhouette) "   "   20
7. Hannah Haskins (portrait) "   "   28
8. Hannah Haskins (silhouette), facing
    page   33
9. The Reverend William Emerson,
    father of R. W. Emerson, facing
    page   38
10. The First Church (Old Brick), fa-
    cing page   45
11. The First Church (Chauncy Place),
    facing page   50
12. Judge William Emerson, brother
    of R. W. Emerson, facing page . 56
13. Ralph Haskins . . . facing page   80
14. The Canterbury House   "   "   85

15. Edward Bliss Emerson, brother of
    R. W. Emerson (silhouette), fa-
    cing page   87
16. Charles Chauncy Emerson, brother
    of R. W. Emerson (silhouette),
    facing page   92
17. Ralph Waldo Emerson (silhouette,
    taken in Concord about 1843),
    facing page   107
18. Octagon Hall, Roxbury, facing page   110
19. The Second Church (New Brick),
    facing page   112
20. R. W. Emerson's house, Concord,
    Mass., facing page   114
21. The Reverend William Emerson's
    book-plate, facing page   142

Ralph Waldo Emerson:

His Maternal Ancestors.

———————

Hanging upon a wall of my study, and looking down upon me while I write, are two old-time portraits. One is the portrait of my father's father, the late John Haskins of Boston; the other, that of his wife, Hannah (Upham) Haskins.[1] These persons were the honored heads of a family of sixteen children, of whom Mrs. Ruth Emerson, the mother of Ralph Waldo Emerson, was the tenth in the order of birth.

The genealogy of the Haskins family is not a long one.[2]

Robert

Robert Haskins.

Robert Haskins, the father of John, is the first of the name of whom there is any trace. He came to Boston in the early part of the last century. His origin is unknown. There are two traditions concerning him. One is that he came to Boston from Virginia, where he is said to have left numerous relatives; the other, that he came from England with a brother and settled in Boston, and that the brother went to Virginia, where there are persons of the name now living.

He married, in 1728, Sarah Cook, daughter of Philip Cook of Cambridge, whose name is on a tombstone of the old burying-ground adjacent to the meeting-house of the First Parish of that town. He lived, after his marriage, in Boston, occupying a house

JOHN HASKINS.

house on the northwest corner of Kingston and Essex Streets, which was taken down only a few years ago. Nothing further is known about him, except that he was by occupation a cooper, and that he died of small-pox during the infancy of his only child, John. His wife, after a widowhood of about seventeen years, married, December 1, 1747, for a second husband, Thomas Hake of Boston, who, like her first husband, was a cooper.

John Haskins.

John Haskins was born in Boston, in the house above referred to, March 12, 1729.

An old and accepted family chronicle records that " when he was sixteen months old, he and his father had the small-pox the natural way. His father died, and the child was so reduced by the disease

disease that he was laid in the same room with his father, apparently dead. By opening the window the child was revived, and spared in mercy to his widowed mother. She was pious, and early taught him to love and fear the Lord. He was an affectionate and devoted and obedient child, and though he wished to go to sea, he determined never to leave his mother until she had another friend."

In early youth he applied himself to acquiring a knowledge of his father's trade, that of a cooper. He was eighteen years of age at the time of his mother's marriage to Mr. Hake.

John now resolved to gratify his long cherished desire to go to sea. He accordingly embarked in a letter-of-marque vessel that was bound for the West Indies and commissioned to act

against

against France and Spain, which were then allied in hostilities against England.[3] He was gone two years, sailing from one island to another, and supporting himself by working at his trade. In his absence he endured many hardships. He was taken prisoner by the Spaniards, and afterwards by the French. He was finally retaken, though with the loss of his clothing, by an American vessel, in which he returned home. He was received by his mother with great joy and gratitude, and was immediately taken into partnership in business by his step-father, Mr. Hake. It is reasonable to suppose that young Haskins's desires for a sea-life had been more than satisfied by the experiences of his voyage. However that may have been, the opening made for him by Mr. Hake proved sufficiently advantageous

tageous at the time to satisfy his
ambitions in staying at home,
and he continued to reside in the
town of his birth till the end of
his long life.

On the twenty-third anniver-
sary of his birth, March 12, 1752,
Mr. Haskins married Hannah,
daughter of Phineas and Hannah
(Waite) Upham, of Malden.
Mrs. Haskins was about five years
younger than her husband. Mr.
Hake died in 1755. By his last
will and testament, dated the
same year, after providing for
the payment of certain legacies,
he devised all the remainder of
his estate, both real and personal,
" unto my much esteemed friend
and son-in-law, John Haskins of
Boston, cooper."

What changes, if any, Mr.
Hake's death made in Mr. Haskins's business, there are no means
of ascertaining. Some time afterwards

terwards, there is reason to suppose that he was concerned in commercial transactions; but this may have been in connection with his business as a cooper. The coopers, in those days, were an incorporated body, and had a large shipping trade, particularly with the West Indies. It is certain that later in life, I do not know when, he changed his business, and was for many years a distiller.

During the period between 1764 and 1769, Mr. Haskins acquired possession by several purchases of a considerable tract of land lying between Rainsford's Lane (now Harrison Avenue) and Orange (now Washington) Street. The front of this property on the latter street was opposite the present Boylston Market. Upon the other end of the estate, fronting on Rainsford's Lane

Lane, Mr. Haskins, in 1765, erected a substantial and spacious house, which he made his home for the remainder of his life.[4] Behind the house was a large garden, with ornamentally paved paths, which is pleasantly remembered by persons still living, especially for its plums and St. Michael pears. In the early years a carriage-way extended through the grounds from street to street.

After Mr. Haskins's death, this house was occupied by the family until the decease of his widow in 1819, and, except for an interval of a few years, continued to be the home of his three unmarried daughters until about 1862, at which time, almost a century after its erection, it was taken down, and the "Savage School" was built by the city of Boston on its site. In 1883, the school-house

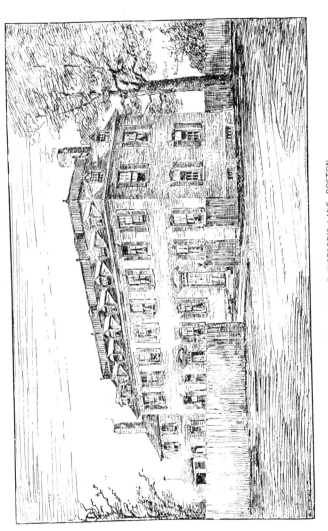

THE HASKINS HOUSE, RAINSFORD'S LANE, BOSTON.

house, having been sold to private parties, was in turn razed to the ground, and a lofty block of brick stores now marks the place of the old family home.

Before the Revolution, Mr. Haskins was much interested in military affairs, and held the commission first of Lieutenant, and afterwards of Captain in the old Boston Regiment. The latter commission is in my possession. It is issued to John Haskins, Gentleman, by Thomas Hutchinson, Esquire, Governor in Chief of the Province of Massachusetts Bay, in the name of his Majesty, King George III., and bears date, Boston, February 20, 1772. I have also in my possession " The Alarm List " of Captain Haskins's company.

In the early days of the excitement over the Stamp Act, Mr. Haskins had been one of the Sons

"Sons of Liberty"; but later, repelled, probably, by the radical measures of Samuel Adams and his followers, he became a moderate royalist. He remained in Boston during the siege; but immediately after the evacuation of the town by the British, he took the oath of allegiance to the new government.

It is not improbable that his father, like most of the English settlers of Massachusetts and Virginia, had been in his younger days attached to the Church of England. His mother, however, who had sole charge of his early training, was a Congregationalist, and brought up her son in her own faith. But in early manhood Mr. Haskins attended King's Chapel, and became deeply interested in the Episcopal church, of which for the more than fifty remaining years of his life he was a prominent

nent and respected member. His
Prayer Book, which has come
down to me, contains his auto-
graph with the date 1757, and,
on the fly-leaf before the Psalms
in metre, a prayer composed and
written by himself, on the occasion of his first receiving the
sacrament of the Lord's Supper,
February 4, 1759. But while he
chose for himself the old paths
to walk in, at the same time, he
never sought unduly to urge his
religious opinions or church preferences upon others. "There
are many ways to Heaven," he
used to say; "but the Episcopal
church is the turnpike road."
He allowed his wife to worship
according to the Puritan forms
under which she had been educated, and made liberal provision
for her doing so, first and for
many years at the New South
Meeting-House, and later at the
Brattle

Brattle Street and the Park Street
Meeting-Houses.

Mr. Haskins took high views
of the duties which pertain to
the head of a family to provide
for the Christian training of the
children. The registers of King's
Chapel and of Trinity Church,
where he worshipped at different
periods, and which record the
baptisms of all of his children,
show the importance which he
attached to having their church
life begin as nearly as practica-
ble with their natural life. For
the most part, the children were
baptized on the day of their birth;
in no instance was the sacrament
delayed beyond the first week
of their existence. From this
beginning, it was his aim to bring
up his family in all the usages
and duties of a Christian life.

When small, the children went
to church as circumstances determined

mined, sometimes with their father to King's Chapel, sometimes with their mother to the New South ; but when old enough to exercise intelligent judgment, they were required by their father to decide for themselves which service they preferred to attend, the Episcopal or the Congregational, and to give him the reasons for their choice in writing. His daughter Ruth (afterwards Mrs. Emerson) was one of the children who expressed a preference for the Episcopal worship. The plan seems to have worked well. It accustomed the children to think and act for themselves, and to hold their religious opinions with moderation and charity. As far as I can learn, the children were very equally divided in their preferences.

It is related that Mr. Haskins and

and his wife, after the latter had
established her connection with
the Park Street Society, were
wont on Sundays to walk together to their respective places
of worship — the children following them in pairs — from the
homestead in Rainsford's Lane
to the corner of Winter and Marl-
boro' (now Washington) Streets.
Here the family procession divided, — Mr. Haskins with those
of the children who preferred
Episcopal worship, turning into
Summer Street to go to Trinity
Church; and Mrs. Haskins with
the others, turning in the opposite direction towards Park
Street. A gentleman, now deceased, who, in the early days,
had been a guest of Mr. Haskins,
and had one Sunday accompanied the family on their way
to church, told me that on ap-
proaching the corner where the
separation

separation must occur, Mr. Haskins gravely turned to him with the enquiry, "Do you prefer to go to meeting with Mrs. Haskins, or will you worship with the saints and *sar*vants of the Lord at Trinity?"

Mr. Haskins was a pew-holder of King's Chapel, and regularly worshipped there till the retreat of the British army from Boston in March, 1776, when the chapel ceased to be used as an Episcopal church. It will be remembered that the venerable Dr. Caner, who had been rector of the church for nearly thirty years, together with the greater part of the proprietors and the congregation, were royalists, and had accompanied the troops in their escape to Halifax. In consequence, the doors of the chapel were closed for eighteen months. During the following five years the

the chapel, with the consent of some of the proprietors who remained in the country, was occupied by the congregation of the Old South Meeting-House. In the meantime, and subsequently till his death, Mr. Haskins worshipped at Trinity Church.

But he never relinquished his property rights in King's Chapel. In 1785, after the forfeited pews of the original owners had been sold, and mostly to the members of the Old South congregation who had long occupied them, Mr. Haskins was appointed, by the then proprietors, one of a committee of seven to report certain desired changes in the Book of Common Prayer. These changes were chiefly in the direction of a reaction against the bald tritheism of much of the congregational preaching of the day. They had already been formulated

formulated, acceptably to his people, by Mr. James Freeman, the young lay pastor of the congregation, in the draft of a revised Service Book. Mr. Freeman had modeled his book, in the main, after the Book of Common Prayer; but not satisfied with the alterations rendered necessary by the changed political relations of the country, he had gone to the length of eliminating or modifying every expression that taught or implied the doctrine of the Trinity. Mr. Haskins took strong ground, both in the committee and before the proprietors, against the last described changes. They were, nevertheless, adopted by a vote of twenty yeas to seven nays.

I have before me two documents relating to the part taken by Mr. Haskins in the above proceedings. One is a manuscript
in

in his own handwriting, of sixteen
pages of letter paper, filled with
proof-texts supporting the doctrine of the Trinity, and with
notes on the origin and compila-
tion of the Prayer Book, evidently designed for his private
use.   The other is the copy of a
paper in the nature of a protest,
which he presented to the proprietors, April 2, 1785, a short
time before their adoption of the
changes reported by the committee.   It is entitled, " Reasons
for Dissenting from the Proposed
Alterations in the Liturgy of the
Church."   In this paper, after a
clear and forcible statement of
his objections to the contem-
plated changes on the ground
that they were not in accord with
the teachings of the Scriptures,
Mr. Haskins urges (1) that it is
unfit and against all ecclesiasti-
cal precedent that questions in-
volving

volving the faith of the church should be passed upon by a body composed wholly of laymen; (2) that a General Convention of the Episcopal Church, made up of both clergymen and laymen, was to be held during the year, by which all needed changes in the Prayer Book would be duly considered and legally made, and by those who had a right to make them; (3) that the proposed changes affected the fundamental doctrine of the Prayer Book, and would, therefore, be unjust to the persons who had contributed to the building and to the funds of the church with the understanding that it was to be conformed in faith and mode of worship to the Church of England.

This document, which is singularly able, as well as entirely respectful in tone, closes with the request

request that, in case the majority report of the committee should be adopted, "this protest may be entered in full on the records of the church." Notwithstanding, no reference to it appears in the books of King's Chapel; nor has it ever, to my knowledge, been brought to the notice of the general public. Later, Mr. Haskins also united with others in protesting against the lay ordination of Mr. Freeman.

Mr. Haskins was over seventy years of age when he retired from active business. He had accumulated a handsome property, which was mostly invested in real estate.

In person, Mr. Haskins was above the common size and stature, with somewhat of a military erectness of figure, and possessed a natural gravity and dignity of bearing, the effect of which was enhanced

JOHN HASKINS, [TAKEN LATE IN LIFE.]

enhanced by his mode of dress, which was that of the ante-revolutionary period.[5] Correspondingly, he was distinguished by unusual strength and uprightness of character, and equally for soundness of judgment and for practical wisdom. Many persons were in the habit of applying to him for counsel in their affairs, and numerous pithy sayings attributed to him were repeated from mouth to mouth for more than a generation after his death. His reputation for truth and rectitude gained for him the popular designation of " Honest John Haskins."

The following anecdote of him was told me by a gentleman who had it from the lips of the elder Harrison Gray Otis. A Boston man, one Mr. John Boies, was on the eve of sailing on a long voyage, and having a few hundred dollars

dollars in silver saved from his earnings, which he did not need to take with him, a friend advised him to deposit the sum in the old Massachusetts Bank. "No," replied Mr. Boies, "old Honest John Haskins is better than any bank; I am going to get him to keep it for me." Mr. Haskins was reluctant to receive the money, but finally yielding to Mr. Boies's urgency, he led the way to the cellar, where he dug a hole in a retired corner in which he buried the box containing the treasure, and placed over it an empty hogshead. Then calling his negro servant, Gloucester, he directed him to fill the hogshead with water. Having seen this done, his visitor departed satisfied. After a long absence Mr. Boies returned, when Mr. Haskins said to him that the care of the money had caused him

some

some uneasiness, and that he should be glad to be relieved of it. Accordingly, with Gloucester's help, the hogshead was emptied and removed, when the box was found safe, and given back to its confiding owner.

Both the devout and the practical sides of Mr. Haskins's character are charmingly illustrated in the explanation he once gave of his preference for a precomposed liturgy in public worship. He said that upon leaving the door of his house to go to church he made it a point, if unattended, to say the service, which he knew by heart, to himself, beginning with the opening sentences, and continuing in the prescribed order, taking both the minister's parts and the people's, till he reached the church. By this course, he said, if he arrived late, he was pretty sure to be up with the minister

minister and lost nothing; on the other hand, if he reached the church before the services began, he was in a better frame of mind for entering upon them a second time.

Still another anecdote has been preserved of Mr. Haskins, which is worth relating for the glimpse it affords of his home life. One day, while the family were at dinner, a building not far from the house was discovered to be on fire. The large group of children started at once and eagerly from their places, but were instantly checked by their father, who, rapping upon the table to command attention, reverently but briefly returned thanks for the meal, saying, as was his wont, "The Lord be praised for this and all his mercies." Then, after a short pause, he added, "Now, boys, run."

In

In business, Mr. Haskins was diligent and methodical in his habits, and scrupulously exact and just in his dealings with others. In the family, he was an exemplary father, faithful and judicious in the training of his children, and a remarkably kind and indulgent husband. His son Ralph, in the entry in his diary which records his father's death, says of his father and mother: "No couple ever lived more happily together during their married life, a period of nearly sixty-three years."

Mr. Haskins was also noted for his hospitable entertainment of visitors, and for his liberal charities. It is said to have been his practice — whether or not it was common in the early days, I am unable to say — to invite two or three persons from the poor-house to dine with him once a year.[6]   Mr.

Mr. Haskins died in Boston, October 27, 1814. He was buried from Trinity Church, on the 31st of the same month, the service having been said by the Reverend Dr. Gardiner.

By particular request of the family, no obituary notices of the deceased, and no mention of the time of the funeral, appeared in the newspapers. Nevertheless, a respectable congregation attended the last rites. The remains of the deceased were placed in the family tomb under the church.[7]

Mr. Haskins's wife and thirteen of his children survived him, besides forty-six grandchildren. It is remarkable that his death was the first that had taken place in his immediate family for nearly fifty-three years, and that for the space of sixty-one years, from Nov. 5, 1761, to Dec. 14, 1822,

not

not a death occurred among the thirteen children who survived him.

The following lines, which were written on the occasion of Mr. Haskins's death by his grandson, Ralph Waldo Emerson, then a lad of eleven years, will be read with interest : —

ON THE DEATH OF MR. JOHN HASKINS.

See the calm exit of the aged saint,
Without a murmur and without complaint;
While round him gathered, all his children
    stand,
And some one holds his withered, pallid
    hand.
He bids them trust in God, nor mourn, nor
    weep;
He breathes religion, and then falls asleep.
Then on angelic wings he soars to God,
Rejoiced to leave his earthly, mortal load;
His head is covered with a crown of gold,
His hands, renewed, a harp immortal hold;
Thus clothed with light, the tuneful spirit
    sings —
He sings of mercy and of Heavenly things.

Hannah

Hannah Upham.

Hannah Upham, the wife of John Haskins, came of good old New England stock, a typical Puritan family. Her ancestor, John Upham, came from England, probably in 1635, and settled in Weymouth; but later he removed to Malden, where the family lived for many years, and where Hannah herself was born. The Uphams were evidently men of ability and character, and enjoyed the confidence of the small communities in which they lived. They were selectmen, moderators of town-meetings, members of the General Court, officers in the militia, and deacons of the church. One of them was town treasurer. Another, Lieutenant Phineas Upham, son of the first settler, was mortally wounded in the great swamp fight with the Narraganset

HANNAH HASKINS.

Narraganset Indians at Canonicus, in 1675. Through her mother, Hannah Waite, Miss Upham was descended from Captain John Waite, one of the leading men of Malden, who was captain of the military company, Speaker of the House of Deputies, and one of the compilers of the first body of the Colony Laws; she was also descended from Rose Dunster, a sister of the Reverend Henry Dunster, the first President of Harvard College; from Thomas Oakes, cousin of the Reverend Mr. Oakes, the fourth President of the same institution, and from John Howland, the famous Mayflower Pilgrim. Hannah's father, Phineas Upham, was one of the ten children of Phineas and Tamsen Upham of Malden, and was born in that town in 1707–8. He was a brother of Dr. Jabez Upham, who settled in Brookfield

Brookfield, and attained distinction there both as a physician and as a member of the General Court. He married, in 1730, Hannah, daughter of Joseph and Lydia Waite. He died in 1738, when about thirty years of age.

The circumstances connected with the death of Mr. Upham furnish a remarkable parallel to those connected with the death of Mr. Robert Haskins, related above. I give them in this case, as in the former, in the words of the old family chronicle: —

"Mr. and Mrs. Upham were both eminently pious. When Hannah was about four years old, the throat distemper prevailed in Malden, and many died. Among these were Mr. Upham, and three of his four children. Hannah, the surviving child, was brought very low. Dr. Tufts
                                    attended

attended her. His remedies were ineffectual. He one day returned from visiting her, and resolved to spend the night in study and prayer on her account, which he did. Finding one medicine that he had not tried, he administered it, and it relieved her. After some time, she was restored, to the great joy of her afflicted mother, with whom she lived alone in the house for seven years. She was carefully and religiously educated, and thus prepared to be a blessing in the church, and to the world. The goodness and mercy of God were signally manifested towards these individuals [John and Hannah Haskins], and the promise connected with the fifth commandment was fulfilled in their experience."

Mrs. Upham, Hannah's mother,

er, married, in 1744–5, for a second husband, Israel Cook, an uncle of John Haskins, with whom she lived for many years, in the family residence at Malden. Their home, during her life, was a favorite gathering-place of Mr. Haskins's family — the daughters going in pairs, to make visits of several days together, to their Grandmother Cook. She died October 3, 1789.

Hannah was born in her father's house in Malden, May 6, 1734; was married in the same town, by the Reverend Joseph Emerson, the grandfather of the Reverend William Emerson who afterward espoused her daughter, Ruth; and died in Boston, September 18, 1819. She was, in many respects, a remarkable woman. Hardly eighteen years of age at the time of her marriage, she became the mother of Mr. Haskins's

HANNAH HASKINS, [TAKEN LATE IN LIFE].

Haskins's sixteen children.[8] Thirteen of these children were living at the time of her death, in her eighty-sixth year, the oldest of these children being then sixty-five years of age, and the youngest forty years. Her health through life was generally good, and her memory and faculties remained unimpaired to the last. The portrait of her, in my possession, painted seven years after her marriage, represents her as unusually slight of figure; but she is described as being, in her later years, a large woman, of fine appearance. She was so far from inheriting wealth that Mr. Haskins, it is said, provided her wedding outfit. But she brought a more than compensating portion to his home, in her singularly calm and happy temperament, and amiable disposition; in the well balanced powers of her mind,

mind, and the strength of her
religious character; in her spiritual culture, and the quiet benig-
nity of her manners. Fully shar-
ing her husband's views in regard to the religious education
of the children, she was peculiarly fitted, by her natural endowments and Christian graces, to
mould their character and guide
their conduct; and, under her
faithful oversight, they were
brought up in the best methods
of a well ordered New England
home. Of the children who lived
beyond infancy, nine were daughters, and naturally came almost
exclusively under her influence.
Their more amiable traits, particularly the eminent loveliness
of disposition which distinguished all of the daughters, are
said, and no doubt correctly, to
have come in a peculiar sense
from her. In what degree the
moral

moral impress of their mother's character manifest in the children was due to their having been so long and closely united in the family bond, it is not easy to determine. But the statistics involved in the inquiry are striking and interesting. The family life, which came to an end at Mrs. Haskins's death, covered a period of more than sixty-seven years. Of the thirteen children who survived her, all were born before the twenty-eighth year of her married life, and till that time only one, the oldest, had been married. Of the twelve others, nine were subsequently married, but at long intervals of succession. The dates show that all of the children lived at home, and enjoyed the influences of the family circle for many years beyond the limits of boyhood or girlhood. The three younger daughters

daughters remained unmarried
and at home through life. The
family intercourse was also kept
up by occasional visits to the old
home from those of the married
children who had settled at a
distance; and, sometimes, these
visits were returned by the parents, in company with one or more
of their other children. There
were, also, weekly gatherings, in
their father's house, of the married children who lived near
home, and during the Christmas
season there were general family
reunions. Though in her later
years the responsible cares of
the household devolved upon the
daughters, by whom they were
assumed in turn, yet, during all
of the period referred to, Mrs.
Haskins was the revered domestic head of the family, the honored and beloved centre of the
home system of thirteen children

dren and nearly fifty grandchildren. Notwithstanding the re-
sponsibilities and cares of her
large family, she was mindful of
her duty to others, and, in pro-
portion to her means, was gen-
erous in her benefactions to the
poor. A pleasant tradition of
the family relates that she kept
a mother-of-pearl charity-box,
capable of holding about five
dollars in silver, from which she
used to draw freely, waving it
before her husband whenever it
needed to be replenished. She
retained her connection with the
Congregational Church to the
last.

At her death, her son Ralph
wrote of her: — "She has performed all the duties of life well.
With truth it may be said, she
was one of the best of mothers,
best of wives, best of Christians,
and best of women." Her remains

mains were deposited with those
of her husband, in the family
tomb under Trinity Church.

Ruth Haskins.

Ruth Haskins, daughter of
John and Hannah (Upham)
Haskins, was born in Boston,
November 9, 1768, and was baptized the same day in King's
Chapel, by the rector, the Reverend Dr. Caner. She was married at her father's house by the
Reverend Dr. Parker, rector of
Trinity Church, October 25, 1796,
to the Reverend William Emerson, minister in the town of Harvard, and son of the minister of
the same name, formerly of Concord. She died in Concord, at
the house of her son, Ralph
Waldo Emerson, November 16,
1853.

Like all of her father's children, Ruth received in her youth
careful

THE REV. WM. EMERSON.

careful religious and domestic training, and the best school opportunities of the day. In addition, it was her happy lot to fill, numerically, the place of "the golden mean," in the line of the children of the family who lived to grow up. She had five sisters and one brother older than herself; and three sisters and three brothers younger. At the time of her birth, her oldest sister was fifteen years of age. The advantages incident to this position in the family were felt more and more as she grew up, and are, no doubt, to be reckoned among the more important influences which contributed to form her character. On the one hand, she enjoyed the society and example of the numerous older band of children; and, on the other, the perhaps greater moral benefit of exercising, on her own part,

part, the tender and responsible offices of an older sister.

Of her life previous to her marriage, I know little, except that it was varied by frequent visits to her married sisters, to her Grandmother Cook, and to her Aunts Waite, at Malden. In these visits, probably, she became acquainted with young William Emerson, whom she afterwards married. His Grandmother Emerson lived there, as well as his Aunts Brinton and Rebecca Emerson, and his Aunts Waite, with whom his sister, Mary Moody Emerson, lived.

It is certain that the lovely Christian graces of Ruth's character had been early developed and matured. The following extract from one of her letters gives an idea of the cast of her mind, and of her spiritual experience at this time. The letter was

was addressed to her sister Deborah, the wife of the Reverend Mase Shepard of Little Compton, R. I., and is dated Boston, June 4, 1793.

"Most sincerely do I thank my sister for her friendly letter by Major Davis, and assure her that with reluctance I let pass the same conveyance of returning her a line. My many avocations, and his stay being short, put it out of my power.

"I was much pleased with your striking comparison of a garden of flowers to the different modes of worship. My sentiments exactly accord with yours, that it depends entirely on the disposition of the heart. May this be but right with God, and we need not fear. For your good and affectionate wishes, receive, in return, the best a grateful

ful heart can offer, for your present and future happiness.

"The contents of Mr. Shepard's and your letters to sister Lydia give me peculiar joy and pleasure. May you go on seeking God, till you obtain at his hand that peace which the world can neither give nor (blessed be God) take away."

The remainder of the letter, which is quite long, is largely taken up with quotations from *Wogan's Essays on the Church Lessons*, which she commends to her sister as a book which she has lately read with great pleasure.

There is also preserved among Ruth's personal papers of this period a series of closely written letter-sheets, in the nature of a Diary, the interesting character and uses of which are explained

in

in the following introductory sentences: —

" Boston, April 20, 1795. Previous to the above date, I have had many thoughts respecting the advantages that might arise from the constant practice of writing down minutely the dealings of God toward me every evening, or at least once a week. Viewing this to be a good means to obtain the knowledge of myself, and to observe if I make progress in the Christian and divine life, or grow in the knowledge of the Holy Scriptures, I desire now in a better strength than my own to resolve that from this date, — April 20, 1795, — I will, as God shall enable me, from time to time carefully notice all his providences towards my friends or myself, whether prosperous or adverse,— and conscientiously

entiously note down whatever appears to be for the glory of God, or the good of my own soul. Most mighty God, assist me now to look up to thee by prayer for thy blessing on these feeble endeavors to promote and strengthen vital piety and true religion in my own immortal soul!"

The entries in this diary are continued, at more or less frequent intervals, until May, 1799.

Ruth was in the twenty-eighth year of her age when she was married to Mr. Emerson. Soon after the wedding she accompanied her husband to Harvard, and at once assumed the charge of his home. Here about three of the fifteen and a half years of their married life were passed, and their first child, a daughter, was born.

Mr.

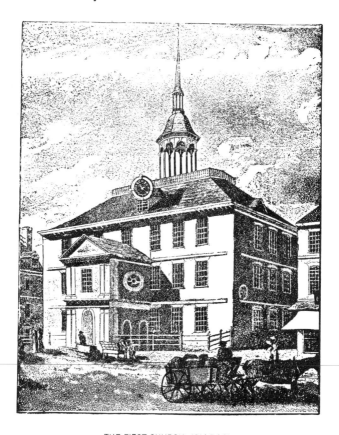

THE FIRST CHURCH, (Old Brick).

WASHINGTON, NEAR COURT STREET.

1712--1808.

THE REV. WM. EMERSON, INSTALLED MINISTER, OCT. 1799.

Mr. Emerson having been chosen to succeed the Reverend Dr. John Clarke, as minister of the First Church, in Boston, the family removed to that town in 1799. There they lived at first in the old parsonage belonging to the church, situated on the southerly side of Summer Street, near the corner of Chauncy Place, now Chauncy Street. Afterwards, while a new parsonage was building on the adjacent corner of Chauncy Place, they occupied for twelve or fourteen months a house in Atkinson Street, opposite the northerly end of Berry Street, which stood next to the house of Mr. Samuel Bradford. But on the completion of the new parsonage they moved into it, and lived there till Mr. Emerson's death.

The following extracts from letters written by Mrs. Emerson while

while she lived in Harvard may prove interesting. They were addressed to her unmarried sister, Elizabeth. In one of these, dated Harvard, April 24, 1797, which was about six months after her marriage, she says: —

" I have ever been disposed to think my affection was the same for each sister; but the pain I feel at a separation from you causes me to believe and own something like to a partiality. Surely it cannot be reprehensible to love so good a sister. But it would be, if I were to repine at our separation while I am under the most endearing obligations to a friend nearer than parents or brethren, one who is altogether worthy of my affections. Thus blessed, fain would I hush every rising murmur about distance from that little spot I once delighted

lighted in as my home, and complain only of those imperfections in myself that render me unworthy of such a companion. I daily regret that so little of that benign and heavenly disposition recommended in the gospel is discernible in my conduct. Our divine Redeemer hath left an example for all those who will live godly lives to follow. Why, then, do we not imitate him more closely? Henceforth, let it be our chief care to walk in his footsteps, that we may be growing in humility and every Christian grace."

The following is from a letter written after her husband had received a call to the pastorate of the First Church, in Boston. The letter is dated Harvard, August 13, 1799: —

" Truly

"Truly, in one view, a removal is not likely much to advance my own private happiness and ease. My partiality for retirement and rural scenes is great; and my aversion is great to the useless ceremony, parade, and pomp, that almost necessarily are attached to a town life. But these smaller considerations are greatly outweighed by the prospect of means for Mr. Emerson's greater improvement in the profession in which he most delights. Consequently, this must render his life more useful and happy. A competency for support without his turning his attention to any other business, joined with the idea of returning to dwell among my kindred and friends, are considerations, my sister, that preponderate in my mind. I am sensible that, with these advantages, my cares will be be multiplied, and probably my sorrows too. Yes, I already begin to feel pain from the consciousness that I am not qualified to move in the sphere of action to which I may possibly be called. My consolation is that the same source remains whence I have derived all that I possess, and where centres all that mortals can wish for, or hope to enjoy. To this blessed fountain, may it ever be my delight and highest ambition to repair, and thence may I continually draw forth such supplies as shall enable me to act with dignity and honor in every station and employment of life."

In a letter dated Harvard, August 20, 1797, Mrs. Emerson pays the following tribute of esteem and love to her mother's mother: —

" We

" We were much pleased with the testimonial of your respect for our deceased grandmamma, whose memory will be ever dear to all who knew her virtues. To you I may breathe forth the wish, for you will join me heartily in it, to possess those inherent virtues, amiable qualifications and graces, that gave the brightest lustre to her character. While we revere and love the memory of our departed friend, let it be our constant care and study to be imitators of her example, as far as she followed our divine Saviour."

Mr. Emerson died May 12, 1811. An entry in my father's diary on the 16th of the same month says: —

" Brother Emerson's funeral took place to-day. A sermon was delivered

THE FIRST CHURCH, (CHAUNCY PLACE),
1805—1868.
THE REV. WM. EMERSON, MINISTER,
1808—1811.

delivered by Mr. Buckminster, and a very large and respectable procession was formed. Between fifty and sixty coaches followed. Every attention has been paid by the committee of the church and its members to the widow and friends of the deceased."

Mr. and Mrs. Emerson had eight children, of whom six, five sons and a daughter, were living at the time of their father's death. The oldest of the surviving children, William, was then hardly ten years of age, while the youngest, a daughter, was an infant in arms. Of the sons, William, Ralph Waldo, Edward Bliss, and Charles Chauncy, were early remarkable for unusual endowments of mind and character. Ralph Waldo was accounted by the near relatives of the family as the least brilliant of the four. Though

Though Mr. Emerson died three quarters of a century ago, yet there is living, and, singularly and happily, not far from my own door, in Cambridge, a lady, now in her ninety-fourth year, who, during her maturer girlhood, was for several years a member of his family, and who has kindly sent me, in her own clear and handsome writing, her reminiscences of that period. The person I refer to is Madam Bradford, widow of the late Charles Bradford of Boston, and mother of the late Joseph Russell Bradford of Cambridge, in whose family she now has her home.

Madam Bradford's letter, which I give below, presents a remarkably realistic picture of the domestic life of the Emerson family. It bears high testimony to the writer's faculties of observation as a girl, and to the extraordinary retentiveness

retentiveness of her memory in age. Her rare simplicity of style, and her facility and felicity of minute description, combine to impart a unique interest to her recollections of the Emerson home in the Summer Street parsonages.

Madam Bradford's Letter.

Dear Sir; I went to reside with Rev. Mr. and Mrs. Emerson in 1806, Mr. Emerson being chosen my guardian. They resided in Summer Street, Boston. I was in the family between four and five years, while the children were quite young. Mrs. Emerson was a lovely woman, very superior and very religious. I do not remember ever to have seen her impatient, or to have heard her express dissatisfaction at any time. The daily duties and cares of domestic life never appeared

appeared to annoy her. She certainly must have exercised great self-control. She was very industrious, and, in order to save time, kept her knitting in a table drawer in the parlor, and would take it out when receiving friendly calls. She had the care of the silver communion plate, and was very particular that it should be made bright before use. I think a man, who was the sexton of the church, came once a month to attend to it. Mrs. Emerson often went to the ironing-board to iron Mr. Emerson's bands. She could trust no one to do them. They were made of lawn. It was the custom at that time for settled ministers to wear bands and black silk gowns, and a plaited, broad band of black silk round the waist. Mr. Emerson looked very handsome thus attired. I remember Mrs. Emerson taking her infants

fants for baptism. She would leave her pew, and alone would take the infant in her arms and go to the altar. Mr. Emerson would take the babe on his arm and baptize it, giving it back to the mother, who returned to her seat calm and undisturbed.

The children when quite young were dressed in yellow flannel by day as by night. I did not think it pretty enough for the pretty boys. But I see now the wisdom, combined with the economy, of Mrs. Emerson. When the boys were older, then dark blue nankeen for jacket and trousers took the place of yellow flannel.

Waldo had a habit of sucking his thumb when he was a very little boy, and his mother made a mitten to his night dress. He sometimes said his prayers to me, the Lord's Prayer, and " Now I lay

lay me down to sleep"; and he often repeated little pieces to me. So did William; but I remember more of Waldo. He used to speak " You'd scarce expect one of my age," " Franklin one night stopped at a public inn," and a part of the " Dialogue between Brutus and Cassius."

Waldo had a wonderful memory. When he was about five years old he went with his father and me to Newburyport. Mr. Emerson went to visit his sister, Mrs. Farnham. I went to my grandmother's, and took Waldo with me. He seemed very willing to be with me. He always called me cousin Mary. We only remained two days in Newbury.

Mrs. Emerson always retired to her chamber after breakfast, for reading and meditation, and must never be interrupted at that time

JUDGE WM. EMERSON.

time. We had family prayers in
the morning, and each one read
a verse of Scripture, the children
taking part as soon as they could
read. Mr. and Mrs. Emerson
were particular as to the keeping
of Saturday evening in preference to Sunday evening. They
never received or made visits on
Saturday evening. At that time
the work-basket was put aside,
the parlor fire-place nicely put in
order for Sunday, and the little
boys' clothes all arranged for
them to dress for the day. Sunday Mrs. Emerson always dressed
in the morning ready for church.
She would often wear a nice cal-
ico. She had a brown silk dress
with a satin stripe which she
often wore when going to a party. I well remember standing
by her when she was before the
glass putting on the lace ruffle
round her neck. I wanted her
                              to

to look pretty, and would sometimes offer a suggestion which
seemed to me an improvement.
I remember going with Mr. and
Mrs. Emerson to a party the
night of the "cold Friday." We
only had a short walk to Chauncy
Place, but it was bitter cold, and
the parlors could not be made
comfortable, though the cheerful
fires gave a pleasant look. The
cold was tremendous.

We had chocolate for breakfast three times a week, with
toasted bread, but no butter.
This has a simple sound, but we
see the wisdom of Mrs. Emerson
as well as economy; for chocolate was better for the health of
the children and for all of us. I
think we always had good dinners. On Saturdays it was salt-
fish dinner, with all its belongings
of vegetables, melted butter, pork-
scraps, etc. The salt-fish dinner
was

was always aristocratic. On Thursdays, which was the day for the " Thursday lecture," the clergymen from the neighboring towns met in the Chauncy Place Church, taking their turns to preach, and Mr. Emerson would generally bring home with him some brother ministers to dine. The sermon and prayer were by the same minister. Old Dr. Pierce of Brookline always set the tune for singing. The congregation rose at the sound of his voice. On the Friday before communion, Mr. Emerson's and Mr. Buckminster's churches united in the afternoon " preparatory lecture." Mr. Buckminster was the minister of the Brattle Street Church. Mrs. Emerson usually attended the " preparatory lecture."

I remember Miss Hannah Adams, the historian, once dining
at

at Mr. Emerson's, with Mr. Buckminster. She seemed to me to be very old. She was short and very small in person, though so great in mind. She became the first tenant at Mount Auburn. The last week in May, which was called " Election Week," in former times, Mr. and Mrs. Emerson sometimes had, on convention morning, twelve ministers to breakfast.

Every Sunday evening Mrs. Emerson had a waiter prepared on the sideboard, with decanters of wine and of some kind of spirits, with tumblers and wine-glasses. The deacons of the church and other friends often came on Sunday evening. Monday afternoons, Mr. and Mrs. Haskins always received their children to tea. I used sometimes to go with Mrs. Emerson. I remember her father as being
genial

genial and cordial in his manners. In the winter time, at the family gathering, he had a silver tankard of sangaree inside the fender, and, when the right time came, he would carry it round that each one should partake of it. They drank it from the tankard. I do not remember much about her mother, except that she was a fine, stately-looking woman. I have a pleasant recollection of Mrs. Emerson's sisters. They were always friendly and kind towards me, and so was her mother. Her sisters, Miss Nancy and Miss Fanny Haskins, were very mild and gentle. I can remember how industrious they were, making tatting and bobbin. I saw much more, however, of her other unmarried sister, Miss Betsey. She was very efficient, and would often come to assist Mrs. Emerson in times of of necessity. On Thanksgiving Day, her father's family all dined at Mr. Emerson's; on Christmas, they all dined at the family home in Rainsford's Lane; on New Year's Day, they met at Mr. Thomas Haskins's, on the corner of Carver and Eliot Streets; and on Twelfth Night, they all went to her brother-in-law, Dr. Kast's, on Hanover Street. I remember what a great privilege I thought it to be allowed to go to these family meetings. They were very pleasant, and without music, or dancing, or games. I remember Mrs. Emerson's sister, Mrs. Kast, as a dignified lady, and her daughter, Miss Sally, who was very pleasant. The latter called to see me a few years after her marriage, with her husband, Dr. George C. Shepard. He was an Episcopal minister, a cousin of his wife, and

and a large, fine-looking man.
It seems to me that Mrs. Emerson's family was a remarkable
one, so respectful and affectionate towards each other. It was
" love all through." I think her
mother must have been a superior woman to have brought up
and educated so large a number
of children, instilling into them
such religious principle that never departed, but has descended
from one generation to another.

I met many years since the
Rev. Samuel Ripley, half-brother
to the Rev. Mr. Emerson, and
on my inquiring how Mrs. Emerson was, his reply quite startled me when he said, " She is
as near heaven as she can be."
I soon understood him. By his
words, we see how he appreciated her pure, spiritual life. I
believe her heaven began on
earth. She was much beloved
by

by the parish. She was a good
disciplinarian, firm and decided
in the government of her children. The law of obedience
must be fulfilled; and when it was
necessary to correct the children,
it was done not in anger.

At the family meetings on Monday the tea was carried round on
a waiter. Green tea, with loaf-
sugar and cream, bread cut thin,
spread with butter and doubled,
with a basket of cake handed
round, this repast was all-suffi-
cient in those days.

Over the sideboard there were
two portraits, one of the Reverend
Charles Chauncy, and the other
of the Reverend John Clarke,
two former ministers of the First
Church, predecessors of Mr. Emerson. Mr. Emerson was a handsome man, with florid complexion.
He was fond of music. I always
am reminded of him when I hear
the

the hymn, "Jesus, I love thy charming name." I think it was his favorite, and I sometimes played it for him to sing.

The new parish house was on the same place where Hovey's store is. Opposite were the large houses of Mr. Bussey and Governor Sullivan, with beautiful gardens. Regretting that I cannot tell you more that would interest you, I am, with sincere regards, Yours truly,

MARY R. BRADFORD.
Cambridge, December, 1885.

Madam Bradford's graphic description of the Emerson home in Summer Street finds a fitting supplement in the glimpses supplied by Mrs. Emerson herself, of the lights and shadows which fell upon one period of her family life. Some of the more characteristic and interesting of the letters

letters of Mrs. Emerson which have been preserved are those which relate to John Clarke, the first of her children born in Boston, who was also, for a season, after the early death of a daughter born in Harvard, the only living child of his parents. The name he bore was given to him in honor of his father's immediate predecessor in the ministry of the First Church. He is said to have developed very interesting traits of character; but he died before completing his eighth year. The circumstances of his death, however, are not given in his mother's letters.

For domestic reasons, which I am unable to explain, when John Clarke was only about six years of age, his parents decided to place him under the oversight and instruction of the Reverend Lincoln

Lincoln Ripley and his wife, Mrs. Phebe Bliss Ripley, of Waterford, Maine. Waterford was one of the homes and gathering places of the Emerson family. Mrs. Ripley was Mr. Emerson's sister; and Mr. Ripley, who was the minister of the town, was a brother of his step-father. Two other sisters of Mr. Emerson also resided in Waterford, namely, Rebecca, the wife of Mr. Robert Haskins (himself a brother of Mrs. Emerson), who had a large family of children, and Miss Mary Moody Emerson, who lived with her.

The letters of Mrs. Emerson, above referred to, were written to her sister, Mrs. Ripley, after John Clarke's departure for his new home. The following extracts from these letters can hardly fail to awaken a tender interest in the little boy, and are especially

ially satisfactory as showing Mrs. Emerson's aims and principles in the education of her children, and the strength of her religious character.

BOSTON, Nov. 16, 1805.

My Dear Sister, I began to write you respecting the important trust we were about committing, for a time, to your care; but ere I had finished, intelligence came that the vessel was just going to sail. I therefore had only time to put Clarke's things hastily into his trunk without a line, or inventory of the articles. Although I feel unwilling to send him at this season, and while so young, from home, yet I know not the persons on earth to whom I should with so much confidence deliver so important a care as that of a child. Oh, my sister, you cannot imagine

agine, because you never experienced, what I now feel! — Having written thus far, I was interrupted.—

Nov. 24, Sabbath evening. A whole week and day has elapsed, and we are still uncertain whether our dear boy has arrived at Waterford. We now begin to fear lest some accident has befallen him on the way, or ere this time we might have heard. But away, all these anxious fears! We have committed him to God, and to you. Your parental care is engaged for him. That holy Being who gives life is able also to preserve it. I will therefore trust in the Lord, and not be afraid, hoping for good tidings.

If the dear child is already, as I hope he is, one of your family, suffer me to mention a few things. The first is, I wish him taught to practise agreeably to the

the Golden Rule, " to do unto others as he would wish others to do unto him"; and make him repeat, if you please, those four lines out of the Primer, "Be you to others," ⁹ etc. I think he understands them. I have perceived sometimes in him a desire to evade prompt obe- dience. I hope he will not dis- cover anything of this sort to you. It is very probable I am myself wholly to blame for this appearance. He at times seems, through indolence, not disposed to help himself to many things which he is quite able to; for instance, if he finds any person inclined to wash and dress him, he will choose they should do it entirely, when, with very little help, he can do it wholly him- self. If he wants a tire or great- coat, he will like to have some one bring it, and I much prefer he

he should wait on himself, and
on others, too, in everything,
that he is equal to. I need not
say, because I know you will
not fail to inculcate on him respect to his superiors, love and
amiable sweetness of deport-
ment to his equals, and kindness
and condescension to his in-
feriors, and to all animals and
insects. You agree so exactly
with us respecting a milk diet
for children, that I shall not fear
his having anything else, more
than once a day meat or broth.

Dec. 1. Again I resume my
pen one moment just to say we
were made happy by hearing
through Mr. Bradlee of the boys'
having safely reached Bridge-
town, and of their meeting Mr.
Ripley there. We are hourly
expecting to hear by letter of
their being at home at Waterford.

On

On Thanksgiving Day, as usual, our parents, brothers, and sisters passed the day with us. . . . Our party were eighteen. John Clarke we missed very much. Give my love to him, and tell him, if you please, I only wait to hear from you that he is a good boy, and then I shall write him a letter as I promised him. In the evening (of Thanksgiving day), at supper table, it was remarked, that, as a family, we had peculiar cause for thankfulness and gratitude to God. For though in every separate family during the past year we have been visited with sickness; yet none have been destroyed by death. . . .

Yours affectionately,
R. EMERSON.

In another letter, dated March 9, 1806, Mrs. Emerson writes as follows: —   "When

" When I was last at Waterford,
I thought it would not be possible for me to visit you again
under many years; but I think
now I shall not be contented un-
less I make an exertion to get
there this Summer, should John
Clarke continue with you through
the season. We are pleased to
hear you speak of his obedience
and affection towards you. Tell
him William and Ralph now go
again to Mrs. Whitwell's School.
His brother Edward we think a
fine boy. This you will say is
very natural, for all parents think
their own children the most for-
ward and promising in the world.
As opportunities are so rare, I
shall send by Mr. Bradlee, a suit
of blue nankeen clothes for John
Clarke, and two pocket handker-
chiefs, with a few sugar-plums.
Give him my love, with a kiss
for me, and tell him it always
makes

makes me happy to hear he is a good boy."

Again, April 20, 1806, she writes: —

"I assure you, my dear sister, we are much indebted to you for your parental attention to John Clarke. However painful the task, we trust you will persevere in correcting everything you discover wrong in him. I am delighted with your resolution in withholding his books as you did, and also with the pains you took to make him humane and charitable. Go on, my dear sister, and . . . teacn him generosity and beneficence, and we shall always applaud your conduct. Give yourself no trouble in future to inform us of the articles you cause him to give; but make him give of those things he values

ues most, till he derives pleasure
from bestowing. I am happy to
hear he is so hardy as to play
without mittens. Give my love
to him, and tell him that I shall
send him a little box, the first
opportunity, if I cannot with this
letter, containing some sugar or-
naments, a Bible, fish, etc., a present to him from Miss Lucy Amo-
ry, a young lady that boards with
us for a little while. I hope I
shall hear he divides these things
with his cousins and schoolmates. I shall send his clothes
for the summer soon, they are
not quite finished."

The following letter describes
the little boy's return to his home
after about a year's absence: —

BOSTON, October 10, 1806.
I thank you very much, my
dear sister, for your letter, and
                                    much

much more for your numerous tender and parental attentions to our dear son. He is well, and appears to have gained much. Truly I was surprised to see him entering the gate, with a young man I did not recollect to have seen before, bringing his clothes. I hasted to the door. He seemed happy, and met me with joy and a tremulous agitation; but did not shed a tear. Information being given to William in the back room that his brother had arrived at home, he came running to the door. On seeing John, he looked amazed till he came half way across the room — as though he could not credit what he saw. They then, as it were in an instant, leapt into each other's arms, and remained locked together for the space of two minutes, kissing each other with great joy. But Edward being

being present did not meet so cordial an embrace from John Clarke. His being an infant when he left home, in arms, and now was running about, the change was so great that he asked if it was not his brother Ralph. On telling him it was not, he still seemed to think it could not be Edward. By and by, Ralph W. came in from school, and John then went and kissed him, and seemed convinced; but did not seem to enjoy half as much from seeing the younger brothers as from seeing William.

. . .

We feel sincerely grateful to God for his guardian care of our dear child in his absence, and for his great goodness to us in returning him in health and safety to our embraces.

Yours affectionately,

R. EMERSON.

John

John Clarke died only about five months after reaching home, April 26, 1807. Mrs. Emerson's affliction was so great, it was not until the following August that her lips were unsealed to her sister. At that time she began a letter to her as follows: —

August, 1807.
My Dear Sister, I have been endeavoring these three months past to bring my mind into such a state as to be able to write to you freely, and to unbosom my sorrow for the loss of our beloved and first-born son, John Clarke. This dear boy is called from our embraces by our heavenly Father, who is infinite in wisdom and goodness. Therefore I will not complain, though I feel daily the agonizing pain arising from his loss, but little diminished by the length of time elapsed since his death. . . .   The

The letter, which is too long to be reproduced in full, concludes, on this topic, in these words: —

"How deeply soever we are afflicted, we know that there is no sorrow we can meet with but some others have felt it before us; and our blessed Saviour himself was pleased to suffer and to die that he might leave us an example of patient suffering. 'In his blest life I see the path, and in his death the price, and in his wonderful ascent the proof supreme, of Immortality.' The most soothing thoughts to our minds under this bereavement, are those that lead us to contemplate our departed child as an inhabitant of celestial glory in the presence of God, his Maker, and associated with angels and spiritual beings, where his infantile capacities will be be continually ripening and expanding through the ages of Eternity." . . .

Mrs. Emerson survived her husband more than forty-two years. After his death, no one stood more nearly in the relation of head and adviser of the family than my father, Mr. Ralph Haskins. Mrs. Emerson was a very dear sister of my father. He was the youngest of the large circle of brothers and sisters. Of the five sisters living at home when my father was born, three were too young to be trusted to assist in the care of their infant brother. Much of this happy charge devolved upon Ruth, who was then eleven years of age. Thus the brother and this sister grew up in peculiar intimacy, and the bonds between them were remarkably strong through life. My

RALPH HASKINS.

My father was married in 1814, four years after the decease of Mrs. Emerson's husband. He made his home for some years in Boston, but, finally, established himself in Roxbury. The Emerson boys, as they grew up, were more and more frequent visitors at my father's house, and were treated by both of my parents as sons. My father had a high appreciation of their character and intellectual qualities. He was proud of their success at college, and, with my mother, always attended their college exhibitions and Commencements. He admired their scholarly tastes and methods. In particular, he cherished great expectations from the brilliant oratorical powers of the two younger brothers. He was gratified by the tender devotion of all the sons to their mother, and equally by their disposition

to

to help one another. He had himself been able to assist in defraying the college expenses of the oldest son, William. But this was all that would be allowed. William, on graduating, taught school in Kennebunk, to enable him to help Waldo through college; Waldo, in turn, kept school to render like help to Edward; and Edward did the same to help Charles. It will be remembered that they all graduated from Cambridge: William, in 1818; Ralph Waldo, in 1821; Edward Bliss, in 1824; and Charles Chauncy, in 1828.

A graceful acknowledgment of Mrs. Emerson's affectionate regard for my father is contained in the following note from her son, Mr. R. W. Emerson. It was written in reply to a note which I addréssed to him some years ago, informing him that I had

had been asked to supply material for a sketch of my father, to be printed in the *Memoirs* of the New England Historic Genealogical Society, and intimating that I should be pleased to receive from him any facts or reminiscences concerning my father that he might deem of interest. In answer, he wrote as follows: —

CONCORD, May 21, 1880.

My Dear Cousin, I have almost ceased to write a letter in my old age, but I must risk the danger at your request. Your father was the admired brother of my mother. I learned from her that I was named *Ralph* for him, he being at the time far absent in the Pacific Ocean, in charge, as supercargo, of one of Mr. Lyman's ships — Mr. Lyman, the then eminent merchant of of Boston. Great was her joy in his safe return home, and he met her affection by careful interest and advice in her affairs from year to year.

His house was to my brothers and myself a joyful place. I recall many visits to it, particularly in Roxbury, when we lived within a mile of you all.

I confess, too, that I was proud of his manly beauty in the "Boston Hussars," and which I think he never lost.

Yours affectionately,

R. W. EMERSON.

I have only a general and imperfect acquaintance with the movements of Mrs. Emerson's household after the death of her husband. The vacancy in the pastorate of the First Church occasioned by Mr. Emerson's death remained unfilled till 1813. For some

THE CANTERBURY HOUSE, ROXBURY.

some two years, or more, of the period which intervened between these events, Mrs. Emerson continued to live in the Summer Street Parsonage. Subsequently, in 1814–15, and perhaps later, she and her family, including her husband's sister, Miss Mary Moody Emerson, made their home with her parents, in the old family mansion in Rainsford's Lane. It was while she was living here that her father died.

My earliest distinct recollections of my aunt and of her sons date from the latter part of the year 1823, when I was five years old. About this time, and for some two years afterwards, the Emerson family, except the oldest son, William, who had lately sailed for Europe, lived in a small house,[10] buried in the woods, in a part of Roxbury, then sometimes called

called Canterbury, situated a few rods up a picturesque lane running easterly out of Back Street, now Walnut Avenue, about half a mile north of the present Forest Hills Cemetery. The house was not visible from Back Street; but from the lane its western gable could be seen above the surrounding foliage. It is to the time of their residence in this house that Mr. Emerson refers in the closing lines of the above letter. My father's home then, and for many years after, was on Back Street, but nearer Boston than the Canterbury house by about a mile, as Mr. Emerson's letter represents. The intervening distance was too trifling to interfere much with the intercourse between the households. I remember that my father's family chaise used often to traverse it to and fro, and occasionally returned with my aunt

to

EDWARD BLISS EMERSON.

to spend the day with my mother. The boys scorned to ride; but their feet brought them at any and all hours to the house. They were the most cheery of the many visitors. They entered with zest into the social life of the household, and seemed equally to enjoy the out-of-door resources which the ample grounds presented. On Wednesday and Saturday afternoons, the woods resounded with their declamations and dialogues.

During the summer of 1824, Mr. Edward B. Emerson, probably at my father's suggestion, certainly with the aid of his influence, established a private school for boys in Roxbury, which both my older brother [11] and myself attended. It was kept in a hall over Field & Gould's dry goods store on Meeting-House Square, at what is now the westerly corner of Highland Street. The school

school was opened by Mr. George
Ripley, acting as temporary sub-
stitute for Mr. Emerson, June 16,
1824. On the 21st of the following month, however, Mr. Edward
B. Emerson himself took charge
of the school, and conducted it
with brilliant success until the
autumn of the next year. At this
time, the ardor with which he had
devoted himself to his work having seriously affected his health,
he arranged with his brother
Waldo to continue the school at
an early date, and entered immediately upon arrangements for
taking a long period of rest.

Mr. Edward B. Emerson possessed in a rare degree that highest quality of a good teacher, the
ability to interest his pupils in
their studies. His enthusiasm for
learning kindled their ambitions,
his engaging manners won their
confidence, and his encouraging
methods

methods of instruction stimulated their efforts to excel. By means of social visits to their homes, and through the abundant opportunities of the school-room, he acquired a knowledge of their character and attainments which enabled him to adapt his instructions to their individual needs. Oratorical talent was much more esteemed and cultivated in the early days than now. Mr. Emerson had won great repute as an orator at Cambridge, where he had lately graduated with the first honors of his class; and parents deemed it a high privilege to have their sons instructed in elocution and declamation by him.

Among the pleasant memories which I recall through the long vista of years in connection with Mr. Edward B. Emerson's school, are two incidents in my own experience, which, though trifling in themselves

themselves, are, perhaps, worth repeating, as showing his ready sympathy with his pupils, and the pains which he took with even the youngest of the boys to make the acquisition of knowledge easy and interesting to them.

I remember that I had one day become wearied and discouraged over my geography lesson. The task required the finding of a long list of towns, rivers, and mountains, upon a map crowded with names printed in very small type. Mr. Emerson, observing that I was disturbed in mind, — I was a child of only six years, — kindly came to my desk, and, having learned the cause of my trouble, laid a wooden ruler which was at hand across the top of the map, and, while slowly moving it down the page, showed me that it was easy for the eye to catch the required names as they came into view

view along its upper edge.   I can
hardly overstate the relief and
satisfaction that I remember to
have received from this simple
expedient.   It taught me to study
with method.   The names on
the map no longer played hide
and seek with me, and from that
time my geography lessons became interesting rather than dis-
couraging.

On the other occasion referred
to, my difficulty was to remember the sermon of which we were
required to present an abstract
during the week.   In this case,
Mr. Emerson happily initiated
me into the uses of mnemonics,
giving me a rule by which, in the
present instance as in the former,
my task was made light and more
attractive.   It was merely to as-
sociate the heads of the discourse
with the columns or windows of
the church, beginning with the
one

one nearest the pulpit, and following them in order as far as was needful.

My earliest recollections of Mrs. Emerson's Roxbury home are associated with the festivities of a large family gathering on Thanksgiving Day, December 2, 1824. I also remember numerous visits to my aunt during the year that followed this event. But I have at hand a more vivid sketch of the domestic circle than my own memory offers, in a letter I have lately received from the Reverend Henry F. Harrington of New Bedford, a Roxbury boy, and one of my seniors at Mr. Emerson's school, where his fine parts were held in high account by both his teacher and schoolmates. Mr. Harrington says:—

" I was repeatedly invited to visit the Emerson family in the ancient

CHARLES CHAUNCY EMERSON.

ancient farm-house in " Love Lane," Roxbury, of a Saturday afternoon and to stay to tea. I have the picture of what I saw at those times in sacred recollection: Madam Emerson, knitting or sewing by the huge old fireplace; the aunt, busy round about in household affairs; and the three talented brothers, Waldo, Edward, and Charles, reading or pleasantly conversing, and making it agreeable for their young guest."

In another part of this letter, Mr. Harrington pays the following eloquent and amply deserved tribute to Mr. Edward B. Emerson: —

" Oh, what a teacher Edward Bliss Emerson was! I have had the supervision of schools the most of my long life. I have been

been familiar with numberless
teachers, and have seen what
some of the best of them have
been and done.   I have had
reason to hold very many in love
and honor as models of high-
toned character, and admirable
service in their vocation.   Yet
none of them have approached
the transcendent reality which
made Edward Bliss Emerson a
gift of God to those he taught.
With conscientious devotion he
threw his whole being into the
work.   He regarded every child
committed to his charge as an
immortal jewel which he was to
free from defiling dross, and fash-
ion and polish for eternity.   So
while with vast intellectual grasp
and ambitions he was earnest for
our mental progress, he was far
more concerned to build up, on
an enduring foundation, the struc-
ture of a noble character ; and
there

there was, withal, the display of a tender sympathy and cheery encouragement which won our hearts.

" He had just graduated from Harvard, and was a model of manly beauty of the highest type in form and feature. His face was the mirror of his inward being. Immaculate purity of soul, intellectual greatness, exquisite refinement of feeling, and tenderest sensibility, were all engaged in limning its wonderful attractions.

" I love to recur to my memory of him. Whenever in the course of my duties I have had occasion to urge my teachers to aspire to emulate a worthy model of excellence, I have only had to describe the reality as it existed in him.

" Had the lives of Edward and Charles been spared beyond early manhood

manhood, the Emerson name would have been still more often spoken. Massachusetts, prolific of foremost men, would have found them among the greatest, at the front in her affairs."

The fact, remembered by very few persons now living, that Mr. Ralph Waldo Emerson, when a young man, had his home for a time in Roxbury, was incidentally but pleasantly brought to general notice by the publication of a letter of Mr. Emerson, written to Dr. James Freeman Clarke, in 1839, and first printed, by permission of Dr. Clarke, in Dr. O. W. Holmes's charming sketch of Mr. Emerson, which appeared in 1884. In the letter referred to, Mr. Emerson, speaking of his verses entitled "Good-by, proud world," remarks that they were composed

composed sixteen years before, when he kept school in Boston, " and lived in a corner of Roxbury called Canterbury." The interest that has since come to be felt in the spot where Mr. Emerson's early home stood is a gratifying tribute to his genius. Dr. Holmes says that "'Goodby, proud world,' recalls Spenser and Raleigh." Mr. Emerson — and notably in these verses — meets the highest test of a poet, in being true to nature. The latter portion of the poem, which I quote here entire, is a strikingly felicitous and faithful description of his " sylvan home."

GOOD-BY, PROUD WORLD.

Good-by, proud world! I'm going home :
Thou'rt not my friend, and I'm not thine.
Long through thy weary courts, I roam ;
A river-ark on the ocean brine,
Long I've been tossed like the driven foam ;
But now, proud world! I'm going home.

Good-by

Good-by to Flattery's fawning face;
To Grandeur, with his wise grimace;
To upstart Wealth's averted eye;
To supple office, low and high;
To crowded halls, to court and street;
To frozen hearts, and hasting feet;
To those who go, and those who come;
Good-by, proud world! I'm going home.

I am going to my own hearth-stone,
Bosomed in yon green hills alone, —
A secret nook in a pleasant land,
Whose groves the frolic fairies planned;
Where arches green the live-long day
Echo the black-bird's roundelay,
And vulgar feet have never trod
A spot that is sacred to thought and God.

Oh! when I am safe in my sylvan home,
I tread on the pride of Greece and Rome;
And when I am stretched beneath the pines
Where the evening star so holy shines,
I laugh at the lore and pride of man,
At the sophist schools and the learned clan;
For what are they all, in their high conceit,
When man in the bush with God may meet!

My father's diary, under the date of Oct. 21, 1825, records William Emerson's first call after his arrival home from his foreign tour, on the 18th instant, and also the farewell call of Edward

Edward B. Emerson, previous to his departure for Europe.

Though the diary is not explicit on the subject, it seems probable that at or near this time Mrs. Emerson removed from Roxbury to Cambridge. I was then seven years of age. But my aunt's form, her lovely sweetness of expression, her gentle manners, just as I was familiar with them at that time, and which impressed every one who knew her, remain the same in the image which my memory now gives of her, unchanged by my later recollections of her in age. This in part explains, perhaps, why the oil-portrait of her now in possession of the Emerson family, and which I remember in my boyhood as an excellent likeness, is highly satisfactory to me, except for a lack of vivacity of expression, largely due, it may be, to the effect

fect of time upon the coloring.[12]

The removal of my aunt's family from Roxbury had its compensations. Though we saw less of her sons, I think we saw more of my aunt than before. Whatever may have been her domestic ties, she was able to make visits to my father's house — often a week or ten days in length — at more or less frequent intervals, during the several years which intervened before my leaving home for college, in 1833. It was mainly from the opportunities presented in these visits that my impressions of her character are derived.

There were no railroads, and, I think, no omnibuses, in those days. My father drove daily in his own chaise into Boston. He never appeared happier than when he returned with " sister Emerson

Emerson" at his side. My brother and I would sometimes run
down the road to greet them.
Her arrival always brought sun-
shine into the household. I do
not mean that she was demon-
strative in her ways. She was
not a great talker, though she
was an attentive and responsive
listener. But there was always
cheer in her presence. She was
sympathetic, and she interested
herself in our home occupations
and amusements. My aunt's visits are pictures in my memory
which I look back upon with
pleasure. But it would hardly
do to attempt to take them out
of the domestic surroundings in
which they are set. Much that
I see in them, while interesting
as bringing to mind my aunt, has
at the same time other and naturally dearer associations; but they
are necessarily wholly personal.
For

For example, my father's home,
especially in its interior life, but,
also, in its outward aspects; the
quiet country road that led up to
it, unfortunate in name, but beautiful with its continuous linings
of barberry bushes, and of savin
trees in some places overgrown
to their tops with the foliage and
brilliant berries of the " Roxbury
waxwork"; the square white
house with green blinds; the
flower beds and green-house and
orchards and green fields and near
woods; to say nothing of the
large variety of animal pets that
were domesticated upon the
premises; for obvious reasons,
none of these things can be ex-
pected to have any general interest. None the less, however, I
can bear witness to the pleasure
and profit which I have received
in various ways through life from
my recollections of Mrs. Emerson

son in my early days. Her lovely character deeply impressed me
as a boy, and I am conscious, if
it has not influenced my life, it
has, at least, been of service in
enabling me to hold up to others
the model of a Christian saint.

The Reverend Samuel Moody
Haskins, D.D., the rector of Saint
Mark's Church, Brooklyn, L. I.,
writes concerning Mrs. Emerson
as follows: —

" Aunt Ruth's face was a benediction to every beholder; her
kind voice, music to the ear;
her kinder words, soothing to
the heart; her deeds of mercy,
a comfort to the sorrowing and
the poor; her memory, a perpet-
ual joy to every one who had
the happiness to know her."

Dr. Haskins's sister, Mrs. Char-
lotte F. Cleveland, of Orange,
N. J.,

N. J., who was a member of Mrs. R. W. Emerson's household during the years 1851–52, bears the following interesting testimony to the character of her aunt: —

" Of an equable, placid temperament, she was ever the same, dignified, yet affectionate to all. She was extremely methodical in all her habits, very much averse to change. She was also a person of great fortitude, an instance of this occurring when her hip was broken during the night, and she would not ring her bell, but waited till the servant came as usual to her room in the morning. It was during my visit that this accident occurred, from which she never wholly recovered. Before this, she walked with us to the Unitarian Church every Sunday morning. During her sickness, she

she wished me to read her a part of the Psalter each day, and frequently the Lessons for the day. Occasionally, on a Sunday, she asked me to read the Communion Service, and requested that her grandchildren should be present. The Prayer Book used was her own, given her by her father, in January, 1783. Her tender thoughtfulness for all was another of her many lovely traits. She enjoyed the visits of Dr. W. H. Channing, who came more than once to talk and pray with her.

"Cousin Waldo came every day to sit for a while with his mother; and, during pear-season, always brought her of his choicest. It was his habit to gather the pears himself every morning — often storing some in his cabinet drawers.

"It was during the winter of 1851–52

1851–52 that Cousin Waldo was helping his younger children in their Latin lessons, which he enlivened in many ways, sometimes repeating fine passages of poetry, with the peculiarly fascinating voice and expression that made it a feast to hear. His eyes were weak, and I read to him quite a number of books, while he would sit with his back to the light. I wish I remembered some of his pithy and pleasing comments. He once asked me how it happened that I had forsaken the church of my ancestors. I replied that I adhered to the church of my father and *our* grandfather. He smiled, and said something complimentary to the Church of England; but I do not recall his words." . . .

Professor Charles Upham Shepard

R. W. EMERSON, [TAKEN ABOUT 1843.]

ard, of New Haven, in reply to a note from me, says: —

"You suggest, in asking some contribution for a sketch of our excellent aunt, Waldo's mother, a task for which I feel quite inadequate. No one short of a Raphael should undertake the portrait of so holy a woman."

Reminiscences of Ralph Waldo Emerson.

Mr. Ralph Waldo Emerson, was born in Boston, May 25, 1803. He graduated at Harvard College, Cambridge, in the class of 1821; was ordained a minister, October 10, 1826, and settled over the Second Church in Boston, March 11, 1829. He married, September 30, 1829, Ellen Louisa Tucker of Concord, N. H., who died February 8, 1831. In September, 1835, he he married, for a second wife, Lidian Jackson of Plymouth, Mass. He died at his home in Concord, April 27, 1882.

The above dates are given only for the convenience of reference. I shall not attempt to fill in the outline with a sketch of Mr. Emerson's life, but only to recall some of the least unimportant of the facts connected with him in the remembrances of my youth and early manhood.

Far back towards the dawning period of my memory — I am enabled by my father's diary to fix the date as the 8th day of May, 1824 — an event of great family importance and interest took place in my father's front parlor, in the presence of the household and some specially invited guests, among whom were my Aunt Emerson and her son Ralph Waldo. The occasion was the

the baptism of my infant sister.[13]
The sacrament was administered
by the Reverend Dr. Gardiner,
rector of Trinity Church, Boston, where the family worshipped; and Mr. Ralph Waldo
Emerson stood as godfather to
the baptized child. Mr. Emerson never forgot this occasion;
but pleasantly referred to it in
what, I believe, was his last
meeting with my sister, in a call
which he made upon her while
she was living in Paris, I think
in 1872.

I have before mentioned that
in the latter part of 1825, when
Mr. Edward B. Emerson was
compelled, on account of failing
health, to give up his school for
boys in Roxbury, he made arrangements with his brother
Waldo to take early charge of
it. In pursuance of this arrange-
ment, Mr. Ralph Waldo Emerson

son re-opened this school, January 3, 1826, in the second story of Octagon Hall,[14] then known as the Norfolk Bank Building, situated on the corner of Dudley and Kenilworth Streets, and which is still standing. My older brother and myself, Mr. Henry F. Harrington, and, I think, most if not all of the other pupils of Mr. Edward Emerson, were also members of this school. I have very agreeable recollections of my Cousin Waldo as a teacher, but, for reasons that I do not know, he gave up the school in less than three months from its opening, or on the 28th of March, 1826. Mr. Harrington, in the letter from which I have before quoted, writing from his remembrances of this time, says : —

" Mr. R. W. Emerson was not
specially

OCTAGON HALL, ROXBURY.

specially successful as a teacher.
He took the school off the hands
of his brother Edward, whose
health had failed. He was study-
ing for the ministry, and his heart
was centred in his studies. Still,
everything went along with the
utmost smoothness, and the intellectual portion of his duties
was faithfully and adequately
performed."

The grief caused in my father's family, by the death of
Mr. Emerson's wife, in February,
1831, was very profound. I had
not myself seen her often; but I
distinctly recall her as a very
beautiful and very lovely person.
Her remains were deposited in
the cemetery situated on what is
now Kearsarge Avenue, Roxbury, a short distance from the
easterly side of Warren Street,
and near the Roxbury Latin
School

School. It was formerly a retired spot, and not devoid of
natural attractions. For several
months after his wife's death, I
think till his departure for Europe in 1833, Mr. Emerson was
in the daily habit of walking
from Boston, in the early morning, to visit her grave. The cemetery lay between my father's
house and the business part of
Roxbury, then known as " Roxbury Street." I often passed Mr.
Emerson on his way to the
grave, as I rode to school. It
used to be said in the family that
no weather interfered with the
regularity of these visits.

My father had early discerned
the promise of the Emerson
boys, and had brought up his
children to feel his own admiration for their character. When
I entered college, in 1833, my
four cousins were all living. At
the

THE SECOND CHURCH, (New Brick).

HANOVER NEAR RICHMOND STREETS,

1721—1845.

the time of my graduation, four
years later, the two youngest of
them, whom I knew best, were
dead; William, the oldest, had
made his home far away in New
York; my cousin Waldo alone
was accessible to me, and he
resided in Concord, some twenty
miles distant from Mr. Greene's
Academy at Jamaica Plain, where
I was a teacher for more than a
year after leaving college. Meantime Mr. Emerson's writings had
attracted universal attention. He
was hailed as a new and great
light. His opinions and utterances were topics of discussion
in all circles. Though I occasionally met him Saturdays at
my father's house, more frequently at his office, in Boston,
where Mr. Emerson had occasion to consult him on his mother's affairs, yet I had a strong
desire to see him in his home,
and

and to find out from observation
and from his own lips as much
as I could of his ways, of his
methods of study and composition, and particularly of his beliefs.

During the vacation periods of
the two years that followed my
leaving college, I found several
opportunities for gratifying this
desire. I remember more than
once driving from Roxbury to
Concord, in company with my
sister, dining at my cousin's, and
returning in the evening. A trivial but interesting point in connection with the dinners was the
form my cousin used in saying
grace before meat. It surpassed
even "episcopal brevity." The
few but sufficient words were,
"We acknowledge the Giver."

Mr. Emerson's regard for my
father manifested itself through
life in the cordial and kind interest

R. W. EMERSON'S HOUSE, CONCORD, MASS.

est which he took in his children. In the earliest of the visits referred to, there were no other guests, and my cousin devoted himself, first of all, to showing us the sights of Concord. In respect to everything that related to Concord he was an enthusiast to the last. After returning to his library I began at once upon the subject I had at heart; begging him as a cousinly favor, which I should highly esteem, to tell me something of his habits of study and writing, and, also, of his religious opinions and beliefs, making, at the same time, playful reference to my attachment to the historic church of our grandfather. He seemed interested and gratified; and with great minuteness of detail answered my various questions. He explained to me his mode of composing. He said that usually

ally, after breakfast, he went to
walk in the woods in pursuit of
a thought; very much as boys
go out in summer to catch
butterflies. He was not always
successful, any more than the boys
were. But, when successful, no
boy was ever happier with his
butterfly than he with his thought.
Having captured his thought, he
put a pin through it, and took it
home, and placed it in his col-
lection. He explained that he
made a note of his thought; but,
generally, only in his mind; and
that he kept what he called a
Thought Book, in which he entered each thought, having first
worked it over and clothed it
in fitting garb. Sometimes he
would go again in the afternoon
into the woods, and there, or
perhaps by the roadside, would
find another thought, which he
would treat in the same manner.
                                But

But this was exceptional. He was satisfied if he succeeded in securing one thought a day. The thoughts were entered one after another in the Thought Book, without regard to their connection. Whenever he wished to write an essay or a lecture, he made free use of the Thought Book, selecting and adapting such thoughts as seemed fitting, and stringing them together as a child strings beads on a thread. After this explanation, I was at no loss to account for the mosaic character of much of his writing.

With equal readiness, and at much greater length, Mr. Emerson answered the many questions which I put to him about his religious opinions. I regret that I am unable to reproduce with accuracy much that he said. I remember that he expressed great admiration

admiration for Swedenborg. It
is not improbable that he was at
that time engaged in writing his
essay upon Swedenborg, which
contains all, and more than all,
that he said to me of him, though
it lacks, of course, the charm
which Mr. Emerson's voice im-
parted to the spoken words. I
assumed, from his enthusiastic
utterances, that he was a Sweden-
borgian. But this he would not
fully allow. On my asking him
how, then, he would define his
position, he answered, and with
greater deliberateness, and longer pauses between his words
than usual, "I am more of a
Quaker than anything else. I
believe in the 'still, small voice,'
and that voice is Christ within
us."

Meeting Mr. Emerson one
day, I think in the summer of
1838, at my father's office in
Boston

Boston, I inquired, incidentally, whether he saw much of my classmate, Mr. Henry D. Thoreau, who was then living in Concord, and with whom I had lately corresponded, I think concerning a school which was in quest of a teacher. "Of Thoreau?" replied Mr. Emerson, his face lighting up with a smile of enthusiasm, "Oh, yes; we could not do without him. When Mr. Carlyle comes to America I expect to introduce Thoreau to him as *the* man of Concord." I was certainly very greatly surprised at these words. They set an estimate upon Thoreau which seemed to me, to say the least, extravagant. In college Mr. Thoreau had made no great impression. He was far from being distinguished as a scholar. He was not known to have any literary tastes; was never a contributor

tributor to the college periodical,
the "Harvardiana"; was not, I
think, interested, certainly not
conspicuous, in any of the literary or scientific societies of the
undergraduates, and, withal, was
of an unsocial disposition, and
kept himself much aloof from
his classmates. At the time we
graduated, I doubt whether any
of his acquaintances regarded
him as giving promise of future
distinction.

But though so brief a period
had elapsed since our college
days, a remarkable reaction —
to use a chemical figure — had
taken place in Thoreau, due to
his frequent contacts and inti-
mate intercourse with Mr. Emerson, beginning from the very
time of his leaving college, and
concerning which I had pre-
viously no knowledge. Social
propinquities have often much to
do

do both in moulding our characters, and in determining our destinies. Thoreau's opportunity did not come to him in college; it was waiting for him in his own village.

Not long after the interview with Mr. Emerson above referred to, I happened to meet Thoreau in Mr. Emerson's study at Concord. I think it was the first time we had come together after leaving college. I was quite startled by the transformation that had taken place in him. His short figure and general cast of countenance were, of course, unchanged; but, in his manners, in the tones and inflections of his voice, in his modes of expression, even in the hesitations and pauses of his speech, he had become the counterpart of Mr. Emerson. Mr. Thoreau's college voice bore **no** resemblance to Mr. Emerson's

son's, and was so familiar to my
ear that I could readily have
identified him by it in the dark.
I was so much struck with the
change, and with the resemblance
in the respects referred to between Mr. Emerson and Mr.
Thoreau, that I remember to
have taken the opportunity as
they sat near together, talking,
of listening to their conversation
with closed eyes, and to have
been unable to determine with
certainty which was speaking.
It was a notable instance of un-
conscious imitation. Nevertheless it did not surpass my com-
prehension. I do not know to
what subtle influences to ascribe
it, but, after conversing with Mr.
Emerson for even a brief time, I
always found myself able and
inclined to adopt his voice and
manner of speaking.

I remember once meeting Mr.
Emerson

Emerson at my father's office, and walking with him to State Street. I happened at that time to be interested in Carlyle, and gladly seized the opportunity to lead my cousin to speak about him. I referred to the difference in the style of composition between Carlyle's earlier and later writings. I remarked that I thought his earlier style a model of excellence, and I asked Mr. Emerson if he could explain to me under what influences, or with what motives, Carlyle had adopted the unnatural, and, as it seemed to me, the affected style of *Sartor Resartus* and *The French Revolution*. It did not occur to me till too late that the question had any personal bearings. Mr. Emerson's reply was partly in the character of a parable. "I presume," he said, "that Mr. Carlyle desires to secure attention

tention. If I had something of great importance to say to the crowd that now jostles us, I am sure I should be at my wits' end to get a hearing. But suppose I should plant a hogshead over there against Scollay's building, and should mount upon it with ribbons of all the bright colors streaming from my hat, and arms, and button-holes, do you not think I should be sure of an audience?"

In the year 1839 I was a student in the Theological Seminary at Andover. Conducted by the classes of that institution is a literary society known as "The Porter Rhetorical Society." I became a member of that society, and was appointed to read a paper before it. I selected for my subject "The Life and Labors of Gibbon."

The following letter from Mr. Emerson

Emerson was evidently written in reply to one from me, informing him of the duty assigned to me, and of the theme I had chosen for my address. It is too stirring an appeal to young scholars not to have a wider application than its writer gave it.

CONCORD, June 18, 1839.

My Dear Cousin, I am glad to hear you have so pleasing and animating a task as a theory of Gibbon's genius. I think a young man cannot read his autobiography without being provoked to rise a little earlier, read a little longer, and dine a little shorter. He knew that every real good must be bought; and therefore, although a man who had as keen a relish as any for literary society and the comfort and splendor which surround the English gentry, he early took the manly part of of banishing himself to a lonely château on the borders of France and Switzerland, where he led among his books a monk's life, compensating himself for the advantages he forfeited, by the pomp of the events and images with which he surrounded his own mind, the whole Roman, the whole barbarian world, and the procession of so many ages and empires. You remember Byron's fine verse to him, Canto III, Stanza 107. And I think you must adorn your essay with the two stately paragraphs in which he records the conception and the conclusion of his history. In the year 1833 I was at Lausanne, and obtained permission of the inhabitants to walk in the garden, "in the covered walk of acacias." It commands a view of the Lake of Geneva.

I do not think there is any need

need to panegyrize Gibbon, nor
to excuse his faults. He seems
to have never forgiven the Cath-
olic Church for having taken
him in, in his youth, and when
once made ashamed of his easy
conversion, he avenged himself
all the rest of his life by his ran-
cor against the whole historical
church. A worse fault is the
dirt he has defiled his notes with,
a cheap and base wit, and no-
wise better than that which
scrawls walls and fences with
its effusions, betraying through
his Greek and Latin a coarse
and mutilated soul, dead to the
meaning of nature, and, in the
midst of what is called culture,
destitute of the highest culture.

But you must give this evil
man his due, and make it felt
what condemnation his noble
labor and perseverance cast upon
scholars who have libraries in
which

which they never read; upon
scholars who chide Gibbon, but
are unable even to name his
dignified studies, his original au-
thorities, his great plan, and great
execution of it. Our young men
read reviews and newspapers,
and smoke and sleep. It seems
to me that erudition is not the
tendency of the best minds of
our time, as it was of Gibbon's
and the following age. We in-
cline to cast off authority, and,
of course, we think instead of
reading. But it at least behooves
those who magnify authority in
this age, to read and know what
authority teaches. The example of this literary iconoclast
ought not to be lost on them.

I have no other words at present to add, and yet, perhaps,
you will warm your own imag-
ination, if you should read the
Belisarius chapters; the chapter
on

on the fall of Constantinople; and perhaps that on Monachism.

Yours affectionately,

R. W. EMERSON.

MR. DAVID GREENE HASKINS, Andover, Massachusetts.

In the subsequent years I had fewer opportunities of seeing much of Mr. Emerson. I occasionally obtained visits from him by procuring invitations to him to lecture before the lyceums in the places where I resided. In this way I secured his presence at my marriage, in Portland, in 1842; likewise in 1851, at my home in Medford, when I was the rector of Grace Church in that town. On this last occasion I remember that some of my people expressed their surprise that I should invite Mr. Emerson to lecture, because they " had supposed he did not believe in God

God." I was probably more successful in allaying their fears than Mr. Emerson himself would have been. Conversing with him at the tea-table, previous to the lecture, I told him of the objection that had been made, and how I met it, which I now forget. I then said to him, in effect: Now, I think I am entitled to ask what you would have answered if the inquiry had been made of you, " Do you believe in God?" His reply, though quaintly worded, was nevertheless very gravely and reverently made: " When I speak of God, I prefer to say It — It." I confess that I was, at first, startled by this answer; but as he explained his views, in the conversation which followed, I could discover no difference between them and the commonly accepted doctrine of God's omnipresence. Conversing lately with my my good friend and neighbor, the Reverend Dr. A. P. Peabody, concerning Mr. Emerson, I remarked that I thought his pantheism was of the best kind. "I do not call it *pantheism*," said Dr. Peabody; "I call it *hypertheism*."

My mind often recurs with interest to one occasion, when, happening to meet Mr. Emerson in Boston, I lunched with him, by invitation, at the American House, in Hanover Street. I am unable either to fix definitely the date of this occasion, or to report accurately, if at all, the conversation that was had. I only remember that on that day he had learned of Miss Martineau's change of views, and her adoption of the dismal philosophy of Materialism, and that I felt oppressed by the dejection of Mr. Emerson's spirits and
the

the sadness of his countenance. The one saw God nowhere, the other saw God everywhere. This is my impression of the explanation he gave me of his dejectedness.

At no period after the early days of Mr. Emerson's residence in Roxbury was it my privilege to live in near neighborhood to him. Even after moving to Cambridge, I seldom met him, except on the college Commencements, and in rare visits in company with some members of my family to his house. But I never lost my inherited admiration of his character, nor my early love of the man.

The last time he was at my house was in 1877. The General Convention of the Episcopal Church met that year in Boston. I had invited the Bishops who were Trustees of the University of

of the South to pass an evening at
my house, and Mr. Emerson and
one or two other special guests
were asked to meet them. Mr.
Emerson came and stayed over
night with me. He was in excellent spirits. The Bishops were
much interested in conversing
with him. Several of them afterwards said to me that their meeting with Mr. Emerson was the
most gratifying incident of their
visit to Boston. The next morning, inviting my cousin into my
study, I called his attention to
the portraits of our grandparents,
referred to in the beginning of
this paper. It was interesting to
observe the pleasure expressed
in his countenance as he stood
before them, and to listen to some
of his childhood's memories of
the "good grandfather and grandmother," of neither of whom I
had any recollection, the former,
indeed

indeed, having died before I was
born. " How well," he said, " I
remember the good old man calling me to him and asking, ' Do
you go to school, my son ? ' —
and when I replied that I did,
his patting my head, and saying,
' That's clever, that's clever.'"

What I have said above of the
appearance and character of my
grandparents, accords with the
description and recollections of
them which Mr. Emerson gave
me at this time.

I was present at Mr. Emerson's funeral; but took no public
part in the services.

The Reverend Dr. Haskins,
who read at the grave a portion
of the Episcopal Order for the
Burial of the Dead, and who pro-
nounced the final benediction,
was the Reverend Samuel Moody
Haskins, D.D., the writer of the
note concerning Mrs. Emerson
above

above quoted, now in the forty-seventh year of his rectorate of Saint Mark's Church, Brooklyn, L. I. He was a cousin of Mr. Emerson on his mother's side as well as on his father's, his father, Mr. Robert Haskins, having married Rebecca Emerson, a sister of the Reverend William Emerson, the father of Ralph Waldo. Dr. Haskins informed me that the Prayer Book which he used upon this occasion was one — referred to above by Mrs. Cleveland — that had been presented to Mr. Emerson's mother by her father, John Haskins, in 1783. He also told me that upon repeating the words: "We therefore commit his body to the ground, earth to earth, ashes to ashes, dust to dust," he threw upon the lowered coffin some ashes which he had collected and brought to the grave from Mr. Emerson's study fire-place

fire-place, commingled with sand
and dust taken from the walk in
front of his house.

With this brief reference to
Mr. Emerson's funeral, my reminiscences of him which have any
general interest come to an end.
Though they are few and incon-
sequential, still, as connected with
the life of so rare a man, I trust
that they will not be thought too
trivial to be recorded.

In the face of an often quoted
aphorism of Mr. Emerson —
"Great geniuses have the short-
est biographies; *their cousins
can tell you nothing about
them*" — it can hardly be ex-
pected that I should attempt any
formal characterization of him.
Besides, I am far from deeming
myself qualified for the under-
taking. The objection, however,
does not apply with equal force
to giving briefly my impressions
of

of the man, which, in fact, is all that the fitness of things requires in bringing these pages to a close.

Considering my early knowledge of Mr. Emerson, it is by no means strange that I should never have experienced the difficulty which many find in accounting for much that appears abnormal in his character and writings. He was endowed by nature, in a remarkable degree, with the faculty of spiritual discernment. His training and education and general surroundings, also, tended almost exclusively to develop the spiritual side of his nature. His mind was thus predisposed to subjectivity, and to concern itself with the spiritual, rather than with the outward, the historical, and objective relations of whatever engaged his attention. Even the predominating faith of New England, in which he had been nurtured

nurtured, and of which his fathers for generations had been among the ablest advocates, was itself based upon a protest against formalism. This was the source of much of its strength as well as of much of its weakness. Puritanism unquestionably had its providential uses in its day. Mr. Emerson was a child of Puritanism. But in his strivings after a spiritual life, he came early to feel that, for himself, all forms, even those connected with the celebration of the Lord's Supper, which Puritanism itself held sacred, were unnecessary — a hindrance and not a help to worship — and he ceased to observe them. In his own words, "Sacrifice was smoke, and forms were shadows." Nevertheless that abounding faith in God, which was the glory of the old Puritans, had struck deep root in his heart and his spiritualistic

ualistic sentiments naturally entwined themselves around it.

I am not aware of any material change in my estimate of Mr. Emerson's character from the time of my earliest acquaintance with him. It is possible, however, that my judgment of him may be, in some degree, unconsciously tinged by my recollections of the lovely qualities of his mother, from whom, it always seemed to me, he inherited many of his most striking traits. If I were asked to express in the fewest words what it was in Mr. Emerson that most impressed me, I should answer without hesitation, his reverent faith in God; his pure and blameless life. Ordinarily, the conversation of even devout men consists with the idea that God is far away from us, governing the universe from his throne
in

in the distant heavens. Whereas intercourse with Mr. Emerson produced the direct reverse of this impression. For his discernings of God were like those of the Psalmist of Israel: "Thou compassest my path and my lying down, and art acquainted with all my ways. . . . Whither shall I go from thy spirit? or whither shall I flee from thy presence?" Everything that went to make up Mr. Emerson's individuality gave unmistakable assurance of this. It was impossible to hold converse with him — I might almost say to hear the tones of his voice, or to mark the expression of his countenance — without perceiving that spiritual things were verities to him, and the near presence of the Infinite One a reality. It was the same conviction of the same

same truth that Saint Paul declared from Mars Hill to the men of Athens, "God is not far from every one of us; for in Him we live and move and have our being." With this profound sense of the divine omnipresence, Mr. Emerson seemed to walk through this earthly life with the wondering tread and rapt mien of one who had been permitted to enter into the streets of the Heavenly Jerusalem; looking on either hand with reverent curiosity; recognizing the divine image even in the humblest of its indwellers, and thoughtfully scrutinizing every object in his way, with the purpose of learning what he could of its relations and uses in the divine economy.

It is impossible that the life of such a man should not be pure and blameless. It is important
tant

tant, also, for the moral uses of
such a life, that the true source
of its inspiration should be
known of all.

FIDEM SERVABO

William Emerson.

(BOOK PLATE OF THE REV. WM. EMERSON.)

NOTES.

[1] These portraits were taken in 1759, seven years after the marriage of the persons they represent, by a painter named Badger. Though open to criticism as works of art, they are nevertheless said to have been good likenesses of the originals at the time they were painted.

[2] See *Memoirs of Ralph Haskins*, by D. G. Haskins, Jr., prepared by request of the "N. E. Historic Genealogical Society," and printed in Vol. I. of the Society's *Memoirs*.

[3] Mr. John Haskins's son, Ralph, says in his diary, under

the date of his father's death:
" My father went to the West
Indies without giving notice to
any one of his intentions, which
he regretted through life."

⁴ The above view of the Haskins house, on Rainsford's Lane
(Harrison Avenue) was produced,
in the main, from a drawing made
from memory by a granddaugh-
ter of John and Hannah Haskins,
who lived there during her school-
days, in 1818, and was also familiar with it in later years. I
refer to Mrs. Fanny Haskins
(Shepard) Boltwood, widow of
the late Lucius Boltwood, Esq.,
of Amherst, Mass. No one now
living is higher authority in respect to either the outward aspects of the old home, or to its
memories and traditions. The
general correctness of Mrs. Boltwood's sketch of the house is
affirmed

affirmed by Mrs. Lydia (Wood) Peverly, who, in 1813, and for some years later, lived in the house opposite, on Rainsford's Lane; as well as by Mr. Ralph Haskins, who, in one period of his youth, was accustomed to visit the house daily.

[5] The late Mr. Charles Foster, of Cambridge, told the writer that, when a boy, he attended worship at Trinity Church, Boston, and distinctly remembered Mr. Haskins's striking appearance as he used to walk up the aisle wearing a long red cloak and carrying in his hand his cocked hat.

[6] Drake, in his "Old Landmarks of Boston," says: "During the Revolutionary War, the inmates of the almshouse frequently suffered for the necessaries

ries of life, and appear to have been at all times largely dependent on the charity of the townspeople."

[7] After the destruction of Trinity Church, by the fire of Nov. 9, 1872, the contents of the Haskins tomb were transferred to Cedar Grove Cemetery, Dorchester.

[8] **The Haskins Family Register.**

1. SARAH, b. Ap. 22, 1753; m. Sept. 21, 1773, John Inman, of Boston; d. Dec. 14, 1822.

2. THOMAS HAKE, b. Jan. 12, 1755; d. Ap. 12, 1755.

3. HANNAH, b. Dec. 17, 1757; m. Nov. 12, 1780, Dr. Thomas Kast, of Boston; d. Sept. 6, 1837.

4. DEBORAH, b. July 17, 1759; d. Oct. 13, 1760.

5. JOHN, b. Ap. 18, 1761; d. Nov. 5, 1761.

John

6. JOHN, b. Aug. 19, 1762 (Harvard Col., 1781) ; m. June 5, 1791, Elizabeth, dau. of William and Sarah (Gardner) Ladd, of Little Compton, R. I.; d. Sept. 11, 1840.

7. LYDIA, b. Oct. 7, 1763; m. May 22, 1798, the Rev. William Greenough, of Newton; d. Dec. 13, 1840.

8. DEBORAH, b. Nov. 5, 1765; m. July 6, 1788, the Rev. Mase Shepard, of Little Compton, R. I.; d. Feb. 11. 1841.

9. MARY, b. Dec. 22, 1766; m. Nov. 7, 1793, William, son of William and Sarah (Gardner) Ladd, of Little Compton, R. I.; d. Oct. 28, 1839.

10. RUTH, b. Nov. 9, 1768; m. Oct. 25, 1796, the Rev. William Emerson, of Harvard, Mass; d. Nov. 16, 1853.

11. ANN, b. Feb. 22, 1770; d. Aug. 9, 1842.

Elizabeth

12. ELIZABETH, b. Ap. 25, 1771; d. March 15, 1853.

13. ROBERT, b. July 2, 1773; m. May 17, 1797, Rebecca Emerson, of Concord, Mass.; d. Jan. 6, 1855.

14. THOMAS, b. Jan. 9, 1775; m. Aug. 23, 1801, Elizabeth, dau. of Dr. Francis and Sarah (Upham) Foxcroft, of Brookfield, Mass; d. Oct. 17, 1853.

15. FANNY, b. Dec. 26, 1777; d. Sept. 16, 1854.

16. RALPH, b. Ap. 5, 1779; m. Rebecca, dau. of David and Rebecca (Rose) Greene, of Boston; d. Nov. 9, 1852.

All of the above named were born in Mr. Haskins's house, in Rainsford's Lane (now Harrison Avenue), Boston.

9 " Be you to others kind and true,
  As you'd have others be to you;
  And never do or say to them
  Whate'er you would not take again."

The

[10] The view of Mrs. Emerson's Canterbury house was produced, with slight alterations, from a sketch drawn from memory by the Reverend Henry F. Harrington, superintendent of schools, New Bedford, and copied by Mr. Arthur Cumming, teacher of drawing in said schools. Its location, as above described, is indicated on Hale's map of the town of Roxbury (1832). The lane upon which it is marked is about one hundred and fifty rods north of Seaver Street. It bears no name. When this lane was extended, it was called Williams Street. It is now included in the territory of Franklin Park. By order of the Park Commissioners of the City of Boston, Mr. L. Foster Morse, auctioneer, Monday, June 2, 1884, sold the house (to be removed) for the sum of twenty dollars. Mr. Morse, in a note

note to the writer giving the above information, says: " The cut of the Emerson Canterbury house is quite correct, and I have had my views of it endorsed by three others who lived in the vicinity for many years." Mr. Augustus Parker, of Roxbury, is authority for the statement that the house used to be called The Parker Scarborough House, and that the late Mr. Moses Williams, who died in 1882, at the age of ninety-two years, said he remembered it as an old house in his boyhood.

[11] Mr. Ralph Haskins, now of New York City.

[12] The albertype frontispiece representation of Mrs. Ruth Emerson was made from a photograph taken from the oil portrait of her above referred to.

The

[13] The late Mrs. Charles C. Jewett.

[14] In Mr. Emerson's day, the tower of Octagon Hall was surmounted by two white colossal figures emblematic of "Charity and her babes," which had formerly stood upon the Boston Almshouse. These were long since removed, but are properly shown in the above drawing of the building.

The book-plate of the Reverend William Emerson, engraved with the family coat-of-arms, represented on another page, is copied from one contained in a small volume which Mr. Emerson himself gave to Madam Bradford, and which she recently kindly presented to the writer.